ISBN 979-8-9878563-8-3

Monthly Planner

Month   Year

Notes & Reminder

Weekly Planner

Month ....

Monday

Tuesday

Wednesday

Thursday

Friday

Saturday

Sunday

Notes & Reminder

....
....
....
....

Weekly Planner

Month ....

Monday	Tuesday

Wednesday	Thursday

Friday	Saturday

Sunday	Notes & Reminder
	....
	....
	....
	....

Weekly Planner

Month ....

Monday

Tuesday

Wednesday

Thursday

Friday

Saturday

Sunday

Notes & Reminder

....

....

....

....

Weekly Planner

Month ....

Monday	Tuesday

Wednesday	Thursday

Friday	Saturday

Sunday	

Notes & Reminder

....
....
....
....

30 DAY Self-Love Challenge

Read a Book for 15 Minutes	Take a Good Nap	Adopt a new good habit	Do your hobby	Go on a picnic
Start a day free of social media	Take Some Exercise	Say no to something	Get a massage	Meditate
Go for a walk	Treat yourself	Listen to an inspiring podcast	Learn a new skill	Catch up with a friend
Define what gives you stress.	Make a bucket list	Set a new short-term goal	Organize your room	Create a self-care kit
Try 30 minutes of yoga	Help someone	Schedule a game night	Connect with nature	Plan out the day
Ask for help	Watch the sunset	Compliment someone	Avoid negative thoughts	Start a journal

Work schedule

Time	
06:00	
07:00	
08:00	
09:00	
10:00	
11:00	
12:00	
13:00	
14:00	
15:00	
16:00	
17:00	
18:00	
19:00	

Work schedule

06:00	
07:00	
08:00	
09:00	
10:00	
11:00	
12:00	
13:00	
14:00	
15:00	
16:00	
17:00	
18:00	
19:00	

Work schedule

06:00	
07:00	
08:00	
09:00	
10:00	
11:00	
12:00	
13:00	
14:00	
15:00	
16:00	
17:00	
18:00	
19:00	

Monthly Planner

Month _____ Year _____

Notes & Reminder

Weekly Planner

Month ....

Monday	Tuesday

Wednesday	Thursday

Friday	Saturday

Sunday

Notes & Reminder

....

....

....

Weekly Planner

Month _____

Monday	Tuesday

Wednesday	Thursday

Friday	Saturday

Sunday	Notes & Reminder
	_____
	_____
	_____
	_____

Weekly Planner

Month _____

Monday

Tuesday

Wednesday

Thursday

Friday

Saturday

Sunday

Notes & Reminder

....

....

....

....

Weekly Planner

Month _____

Monday

Tuesday

Wednesday

Thursday

Friday

Saturday

Sunday

Notes & Reminder

_____
_____
_____
_____

Work schedule

06:00	
07:00	
08:00	
09:00	
10:00	
11:00	
12:00	
13:00	
14:00	
15:00	
16:00	
17:00	
18:00	
19:00	

Work schedule

06:00	
07:00	
08:00	
09:00	
10:00	
11:00	
12:00	
13:00	
14:00	
15:00	
16:00	
17:00	
18:00	
19:00	

Work schedule

Time	
06:00	
07:00	
08:00	
09:00	
10:00	
11:00	
12:00	
13:00	
14:00	
15:00	
16:00	
17:00	
18:00	
19:00	

Work schedule

06:00	
07:00	
08:00	
09:00	
10:00	
11:00	
12:00	
13:00	
14:00	
15:00	
16:00	
17:00	
18:00	
19:00	

Monthly Planner

Month   Year

Notes & Reminder

Weekly Planner

Month _____

Monday

Tuesday

Wednesday

Thursday

Friday

Saturday

Sunday

Notes & Reminder

....

....

....

....

Weekly Planner

Month _____

Monday

Tuesday

Wednesday

Thursday

Friday

Saturday

Sunday

Notes & Reminder

_____

_____

_____

_____

Weekly Planner

Month ....

Monday

Tuesday

Wednesday

Thursday

Friday

Saturday

Sunday

Notes & Reminder

....

....

....

....

Weekly Planner

Month ....

Monday	Tuesday

Wednesday	Thursday

Friday	Saturday

Sunday	Notes & Reminder
	....
	....
	....
	....

Work schedule

Time	
06:00	
07:00	
08:00	
09:00	
10:00	
11:00	
12:00	
13:00	
14:00	
15:00	
16:00	
17:00	
18:00	
19:00	

Work schedule

06:00	
07:00	
08:00	
09:00	
10:00	
11:00	
12:00	
13:00	
14:00	
15:00	
16:00	
17:00	
18:00	
19:00	

Work schedule

06:00	
07:00	
08:00	
09:00	
10:00	
11:00	
12:00	
13:00	
14:00	
15:00	
16:00	
17:00	
18:00	
19:00	

Monthly Planner

Month   Year

Notes & Reminder

Weekly Planner

Month ....

Monday

Tuesday

Wednesday

Thursday

Friday

Saturday

Sunday

Notes & Reminder

....

....

....

....

Weekly Planner

Month _____

Monday

Tuesday

Wednesday

Thursday

Friday

Saturday

Sunday

Notes & Reminder

_____
_____
_____
_____

Weekly Planner

Month _____

Monday

Tuesday

Wednesday

Thursday

Friday

Saturday

Sunday

Notes & Reminder

....

....

....

....

Weekly Planner

Month ....

Monday

Tuesday

Wednesday

Thursday

Friday

Saturday

Sunday

Notes & Reminder

....
....
....
....

Work schedule

06:00	
07:00	
08:00	
09:00	
10:00	
11:00	
12:00	
13:00	
14:00	
15:00	
16:00	
17:00	
18:00	
19:00	

Work schedule

06:00	
07:00	
08:00	
09:00	
10:00	
11:00	
12:00	
13:00	
14:00	
15:00	
16:00	
17:00	
18:00	
19:00	

Work schedule

06:00	
07:00	
08:00	
09:00	
10:00	
11:00	
12:00	
13:00	
14:00	
15:00	
16:00	
17:00	
18:00	
19:00	

Monthly Planner

Month _____ Year _____

Notes & Reminder

Weekly Planner

Month _____

Monday

Tuesday

Wednesday

Thursday

Friday

Saturday

Sunday

Notes & Reminder

_____

_____

_____

_____

Weekly Planner

Month _____

Monday

Tuesday

Wednesday

Thursday

Friday

Saturday

Sunday

Notes & Reminder

_____
_____
_____
_____

Weekly Planner

Month ....

Monday

Tuesday

Wednesday

Thursday

Friday

Saturday

Sunday

Notes & Reminder

....
....
....
....

Weekly Planner

Month ....

Monday

Tuesday

Wednesday

Thursday

Friday

Saturday

Sunday

Notes & Reminder

....
....
....
....

Work schedule

06:00	
07:00	
08:00	
09:00	
10:00	
11:00	
12:00	
13:00	
14:00	
15:00	
16:00	
17:00	
18:00	
19:00	

Work schedule

06:00	
07:00	
08:00	
09:00	
10:00	
11:00	
12:00	
13:00	
14:00	
15:00	
16:00	
17:00	
18:00	
19:00	

Work schedule

06:00	
07:00	
08:00	
09:00	
10:00	
11:00	
12:00	
13:00	
14:00	
15:00	
16:00	
17:00	
18:00	
19:00	

Monthly Planner

Month _____ Year _____

Notes & Reminder

Weekly Planner

Month ....

Monday

Tuesday

Wednesday

Thursday

Friday

Saturday

Sunday

Notes & Reminder

....
....
....
....

Weekly Planner

Month _____

Monday

Tuesday

Wednesday

Thursday

Friday

Saturday

Sunday

Notes & Reminder

_____
_____
_____
_____

Weekly Planner

Month _____

Monday

Tuesday

Wednesday

Thursday

Friday

Saturday

Sunday

Notes & Reminder

....

....

....

....

Weekly Planner

Month ....

Monday

Tuesday

Wednesday

Thursday

Friday

Saturday

Sunday

Notes & Reminder

....
....
....
....

Weekly Planner

Month _____

Monday

Tuesday

Wednesday

Thursday

Friday

Saturday

Sunday

Notes & Reminder

_____
_____
_____
_____

Work schedule

Time	
06:00	
07:00	
08:00	
09:00	
10:00	
11:00	
12:00	
13:00	
14:00	
15:00	
16:00	
17:00	
18:00	
19:00	

Work schedule

Time	
06:00	
07:00	
08:00	
09:00	
10:00	
11:00	
12:00	
13:00	
14:00	
15:00	
16:00	
17:00	
18:00	
19:00	

Work schedule

06:00	
07:00	
08:00	
09:00	
10:00	
11:00	
12:00	
13:00	
14:00	
15:00	
16:00	
17:00	
18:00	
19:00	

Work schedule

06:00	
07:00	
08:00	
09:00	
10:00	
11:00	
12:00	
13:00	
14:00	
15:00	
16:00	
17:00	
18:00	
19:00	

Monthly Planner

Month   Year

Notes & Reminder

Weekly Planner

Month_____

Monday

Tuesday

Wednesday

Thursday

Friday

Saturday

Sunday

Notes & Reminder

....

....

....

....

Weekly Planner

Month ....

Monday

Tuesday

Wednesday

Thursday

Friday

Saturday

Sunday

Notes & Reminder

....
....
....
....

Weekly Planner

Month ....

Monday

Tuesday

Wednesday

Thursday

Friday

Saturday

Sunday

Notes & Reminder

....
....
....
....

Weekly Planner

Month ....

Monday

Tuesday

Wednesday

Thursday

Friday

Saturday

Sunday

Notes & Reminder

....

....

....

....

Work schedule

Time	
06:00	
07:00	
08:00	
09:00	
10:00	
11:00	
12:00	
13:00	
14:00	
15:00	
16:00	
17:00	
18:00	
19:00	

Work schedule

06:00

07:00

08:00

09:00

10:00

11:00

12:00

13:00

14:00

15:00

16:00

17:00

18:00

19:00

Work schedule

06:00	
07:00	
08:00	
09:00	
10:00	
11:00	
12:00	
13:00	
14:00	
15:00	
16:00	
17:00	
18:00	
19:00	

Monthly Planner

Month _____ Year _____

Weekly Planner

Month _____

Monday

Tuesday

Wednesday

Thursday

Friday

Saturday

Sunday

Notes & Reminder

_____
_____
_____
_____

Weekly Planner

Month ....

Monday

Tuesday

Wednesday

Thursday

Friday

Saturday

Sunday

Notes & Reminder

....
....
....
....

Weekly Planner

Month _____

Monday

Tuesday

Wednesday

Thursday

Friday

Saturday

Sunday

Notes & Reminder

_____

_____

_____

_____

Weekly Planner

Month ....

Monday

Tuesday

Wednesday

Thursday

Friday

Saturday

Sunday

Notes & Reminder

....

....

....

....

Work schedule

06:00	
07:00	
08:00	
09:00	
10:00	
11:00	
12:00	
13:00	
14:00	
15:00	
16:00	
17:00	
18:00	
19:00	

Work schedule

06:00

07:00

08:00

09:00

10:00

11:00

12:00

13:00

14:00

15:00

16:00

17:00

18:00

19:00

Work schedule

06:00	
07:00	
08:00	
09:00	
10:00	
11:00	
12:00	
13:00	
14:00	
15:00	
16:00	
17:00	
18:00	
19:00	

Monthly Planner

Month   Year

Notes & Reminder

Weekly Planner

Month _____

Monday

Tuesday

Wednesday

Thursday

Friday

Saturday

Sunday

Notes & Reminder

_____
_____
_____
_____

Weekly Planner

Month ....

Monday

Tuesday

Wednesday

Thursday

Friday

Saturday

Sunday

Notes & Reminder

....
....
....
....

Weekly Planner

Month _____

Monday

Tuesday

Wednesday

Thursday

Friday

Saturday

Sunday

Notes & Reminder
_____
_____
_____
_____

Weekly Planner

Month ....

Monday

Tuesday

Wednesday

Thursday

Friday

Saturday

Sunday

Notes & Reminder

....

....

....

....

Work schedule

06:00	
07:00	
08:00	
09:00	
10:00	
11:00	
12:00	
13:00	
14:00	
15:00	
16:00	
17:00	
18:00	
19:00	

Work schedule

06:00	
07:00	
08:00	
09:00	
10:00	
11:00	
12:00	
13:00	
14:00	
15:00	
16:00	
17:00	
18:00	
19:00	

Work schedule

06:00	
07:00	
08:00	
09:00	
10:00	
11:00	
12:00	
13:00	
14:00	
15:00	
16:00	
17:00	
18:00	
19:00	

Monthly Planner

Month _____ Year _____

Weekly Planner

Month ....

Monday

Tuesday

Wednesday

Thursday

Friday

Saturday

Sunday

Notes & Reminder

....

....

....

....

Weekly Planner

Month ....

Monday

Tuesday

Wednesday

Thursday

Friday

Saturday

Sunday

Notes & Reminder

....
....
....
....

Weekly Planner

Month _____

Monday

Tuesday

Wednesday

Thursday

Friday

Saturday

Sunday

Notes & Reminder

_____
_____
_____
_____

Weekly Planner

Month ....

Monday

Tuesday

Wednesday

Thursday

Friday

Saturday

Sunday

Notes & Reminder

....

....

....

....

Weekly Planner

Month _____

Monday	Tuesday

Wednesday	Thursday

Friday	Saturday

Sunday	Notes & Reminder
	....
	....
	....

Work schedule

Time	
06:00	
07:00	
08:00	
09:00	
10:00	
11:00	
12:00	
13:00	
14:00	
15:00	
16:00	
17:00	
18:00	
19:00	

Work schedule

Time	
06:00	
07:00	
08:00	
09:00	
10:00	
11:00	
12:00	
13:00	
14:00	
15:00	
16:00	
17:00	
18:00	
19:00	

Work schedule

06:00	
07:00	
08:00	
09:00	
10:00	
11:00	
12:00	
13:00	
14:00	
15:00	
16:00	
17:00	
18:00	
19:00	

Work schedule

06:00	
07:00	
08:00	
09:00	
10:00	
11:00	
12:00	
13:00	
14:00	
15:00	
16:00	
17:00	
18:00	
19:00	

Monthly Planner

Month   Year

Notes & Reminder

Weekly Planner

Month _____

Monday

Tuesday

Wednesday

Thursday

Friday

Saturday

Sunday

Notes & Reminder

....
....
....
....

Weekly Planner

Month _____

Monday

Tuesday

Wednesday

Thursday

Friday

Saturday

Sunday

Notes & Reminder

_____
_____
_____
_____

Weekly Planner

Month ....

Monday

Tuesday

Wednesday

Thursday

Friday

Saturday

Sunday

Notes & Reminder

....
....
....
....

Weekly Planner

Month _____

Monday	Tuesday

Wednesday	Thursday

Friday	Saturday

Sunday

Notes & Reminder

....

....

....

....

Work schedule

06:00	
07:00	
08:00	
09:00	
10:00	
11:00	
12:00	
13:00	
14:00	
15:00	
16:00	
17:00	
18:00	
19:00	

Work schedule

06:00	
07:00	
08:00	
09:00	
10:00	
11:00	
12:00	
13:00	
14:00	
15:00	
16:00	
17:00	
18:00	
19:00	

Work schedule

Time	
06:00	
07:00	
08:00	
09:00	
10:00	
11:00	
12:00	
13:00	
14:00	
15:00	
16:00	
17:00	
18:00	
19:00	

Monthly Planner

Month _____   Year _____

Notes & Reminder

Weekly Planner

Month _____

Monday

Tuesday

Wednesday

Thursday

Friday

Saturday

Sunday

Notes & Reminder

_____

_____

_____

_____

Weekly Planner

Month _____

Monday

Tuesday

Wednesday

Thursday

Friday

Saturday

Sunday

Notes & Reminder

_____
_____
_____
_____

Weekly Planner

Month _____

Monday

Tuesday

Wednesday

Thursday

Friday

Saturday

Sunday

Notes & Reminder

_____
_____
_____
_____

Weekly Planner

Month ....

Monday	Tuesday

Wednesday	Thursday

Friday	Saturday

Sunday	Notes & Reminder
	....
	....
	....
	....

Work schedule

Time	
06:00	
07:00	
08:00	
09:00	
10:00	
11:00	
12:00	
13:00	
14:00	
15:00	
16:00	
17:00	
18:00	
19:00	

Work schedule

Time	
06:00	
07:00	
08:00	
09:00	
10:00	
11:00	
12:00	
13:00	
14:00	
15:00	
16:00	
17:00	
18:00	
19:00	

Work schedule

Time	
06:00	
07:00	
08:00	
09:00	
10:00	
11:00	
12:00	
13:00	
14:00	
15:00	
16:00	
17:00	
18:00	
19:00	

Monthly Planner

Month _____ Year _____

Notes & Reminder

Weekly Planner

Month _____

Monday

Tuesday

Wednesday

Thursday

Friday

Saturday

Sunday

Notes & Reminder

_____
_____
_____
_____

Weekly Planner

Month _____

Monday

Tuesday

Wednesday

Thursday

Friday

Saturday

Sunday

Notes & Reminder

_____

_____

_____

_____

Weekly Planner

Month ....

Monday

Tuesday

Wednesday

Thursday

Friday

Saturday

Sunday

Notes & Reminder

....

....

....

....

Weekly Planner

Month ....

Monday	Tuesday
Wednesday	Thursday
Friday	Saturday

Sunday

Notes & Reminder

....

....

....

....

Work schedule

Time	
06:00	
07:00	
08:00	
09:00	
10:00	
11:00	
12:00	
13:00	
14:00	
15:00	
16:00	
17:00	
18:00	
19:00	

Work schedule

06:00	
07:00	
08:00	
09:00	
10:00	
11:00	
12:00	
13:00	
14:00	
15:00	
16:00	
17:00	
18:00	
19:00	

Work schedule

Time	
06:00	
07:00	
08:00	
09:00	
10:00	
11:00	
12:00	
13:00	
14:00	
15:00	
16:00	
17:00	
18:00	
19:00	

www.ingramcontent.com/pod-product-compliance
Lightning Source LLC
Chambersburg PA
CBHW081419090426
42738CB00017B/3416